Any Reason To Smile Will Do

Caroline Sands

BookLeaf Publishing

Presentation by *BookLeaf Publishing*

Web: www.bookleafpub.com

E-mail: info@bookleafpub.com

ISBN: 9789358312935

First edition 2023

ACKNOWLEDGEMENT

I will always want to send my appreciation to my parents who adopted me as a baby and stood by my side through every struggle I had.
The number one acknowledgement I want to give is to all of my family and friends who have watched and stood by my side, thank you.

John, Eileen, Kathleen, Daniel, Frank, Arlene, Katherine, Jim, Kevin, Paul, Jeanne, Carol, Devin, Dillon, Josh, Jack, Vincent, Bandit, Rascal, Iggy, Scamp, Ruffian, Luna, Maggie, Cassia, Meghan, Leia, Taz, Tazman, Louis Tedstone, Whiskey Fransisco, Thumper, Zoots, Speedy, Cassie, and many more who I respect in my heart so much and they know this.
My beating reason for my smile each day I want to thank my lucky catch from this sea. The man like no other. I love you and never stop driving towards what you believe in. You do you the best. And you know that all too well.

PREFACE

Being the best person walking out of my door into the world is my goal on any day. I can only hope if I teach anyone one thing, the three second rule should be for driving on the road. I almost died so many times in my life, and this is the number one lesson I still use in my daily life that saves me stress and time. Three seconds behind and there's always going to be space to see and react on time.

Table of contents:

Truth Be Told

Depression is a constant sugar mountain on a sunny day
When the weatherman promised we would have a cloud-free day
As long as we take our umbrella with us each day.

Protecting ourselves with a false safety net is what this says.
Take some pills to hide your pain.
Cover your scars with makeup to forget where you have been.
Hide your shame in fancy suits and gowns while you parade around town.

If I asked how many have lived and had the profound ability to not tell a lie?

No, honestly, I know that I am not the only one.
Please.
Tell me there are others who have been hurt by the truth and know to still speak it.
Tell me there are others who know the value of their words.

Plain Poem

Living life is all a time evaluating equation of choices.
When one step is made, every day, we are deciding.

Micro choices that eventually create our aura that is us.
And wheather or not that leads us to be of a value or a danger
Will only be for our scrolls to unfold to tell the truth.

Makeup on our faces will never truly help us win any race
Nor can it engage in earning hard yearned for respect.

World wide fear is consuming all at paces unheard

And the earth was mainly designed to walk on
the plains.

We had grown bored of the plains we roamed.
Curiosity got to us.
We decided to embrace the cats. We grew our
greed and fed the need.

What did we not do?
Care for ourselves as a unity?
What was the declaration for if we are still so
inner intrigued by wars outdoors?

It's as if we are backtracking to kindergarten
when we would rather place our funds
In the ideas of ending lives?
Why is hatred the most powerful emotion to take
our minds away from ourselves?
Why can fear take the ability to see clear and
starve us blind in a puddle of mud?

Can we free ourselves? Would a helping hand
even help now?

I fear. You fear. We all fear for our final scream
for no reason could prepare anyone for a total
loss.

Thinking before anything is too far lost may be
the best hope for another day.

As the sun will come up tomorrow.
The sun never comes up as the song goes
though.
We revolve around the sun like the barrel of a
gun.
We will never see ourselves win for we will trip
the wind before bowing to the rain in vain.

Foolish is our hypocrisy in all of societies'
displaced ignorant intolerance.

Race, weight, intellectual abilities.
Gender, appearance, Health.

Many bully others for fun as they have some
advantage over the other
And when we finally can step back to look at the
planet.
No one advantage will lead anyone anywhere
sooner or later than anyone else.

If we are all decided on being blind and
oblivious to our actions daily, well,
When we consume ourselves with our own
confusion leading to mass delusions,
That's when we all lose.

Blindly winning in our minds though is all of most importance.

We win on the highway as we race faster to stop the traffic from merging in
Though law enforcement advises legally that merge one must if obstruction
Is on the road though does anyone realize the dangers of their action

Short Story

A space in time is where we start. Is now 8 hours since the moon rose and filled all the sky with the magnificent glow that has bestowed our journey's guidance. Pleasantly, I and 3 other travelers were going on a quest to find the most satisfying and rewarding treasure anyone could dream of.

My buddies and I all loved to 'par-core' our way around our environment. As the moon was traveling with us, we would see it reflecting through the waterlogged puddles in the roads, the lakes still as the night and as well in the windows that were all bunkered closed due to

the shivering brisk night air filling the countryside.
It was our favorite weather and the best time for us young ones to get mischievous and have least chances of any dangers. Truly, we often found that we were our own biggest threat time and time again. We will never be able to live down the time we blew the bridge up by knocking the milk bottles out of the truck and causing the truck to crash into a telephone pole that blew its transmitter box and ignited the field in blazes of glory. All for what? We did have the worst belly aches after that feast and fiasco.
Terrible events seem to follow us just like that waving thing on the back side of each of us. We still don't know why we are always saying hi. Even to ourselves. We turn around and say hi to our own faces and then hi ourselves back. It's a routine that still never tires from its enjoyability though.
Turning down the trail we all see a hungry looking beast who looks snappier than any hunter could ever hope. We were scared as a whistle without any air to blow. We couldn't run anymore for the dangers behind were greatest when the moon was gone, and the sun shone bright. Their best option was to pass straight forward.
Oh, and how were they to do this?

One said to the other and they all whispered the idea onto the next. Once their plan was agreed upon and details fine-tuned, they scattered off in four different directions. Their foe was so stunned he sat down where he had first seen his enemies, and this was now the same exact spot where he last saw us as well. We were not about to become lunch. Dog meat we are not, for sure! By just before the moon fully dropped down into the low rinks of the sky, the sun was starting to peak over the opposing horizon. Perfect timing. Maybe we all have heard the sayings of the early birds catching the worm. Well, us on the other hand, we use our south paws to clamber the daylight out of those sun-loving birds like it's a wack-a-mole arena and it's almost always chalked up as one for fun. We just can't stand those wings of vibration and energy and color and gosh, why are birds such spazzing creatures of chaos?

The best play is when we can all collaborate to compete and succeed as one unit. Patrolling is our specialty. The four amigos we could best be referred to. Lox, Wanker, Critter and Mur. We are all cats. All mischievous, furry, adorable creatures with a hidden desire to kill any creature that moves faster than we can process our own thoughts or eyes. If we have the striking moment, with pleasure, our paw goes up and comes back down.

Nighttime is our best friend and that's for the cover it gives to hide our day's deeds.

Sometimes we bring a present home if we are in a giving mood and not too lazy to carry baggage on our return.

Double War

Naso
Hooked cross.
Fertility
Good fortune
Loss of time
Demand
Demand
Radio waves
Death to planes with radio airwaves.
Not quite
But sonar a might
Peace or mislead.
Non-aggression pact broken.
Comes as no shocking alarm.
As 70,000 breaths end
And 50,000 more flies from opposing sides.
"Mon Diue" Hitler cries as soldiers' eyes
Led the march across Europe.

As world starts to watch when France began
Weakening strengths along the
Mahjino Line
Luxemburg and Belgium
With tanks and planes
Devastating like no lives were worth wondering why.
As if life meant nothing as bones and guts,
Lead into front line and left feeling alone.
Watching closely for overhead tones.
As if they were sent to bleed out as bait.
With orders to charge and wait.
Are we fish in a sea like measly chum thrown to shark?
When we hunt for fins, food, fame or fun.
When we, if we, grow to be old and decrepit,
Cracked inside long ago that still cracks today the same way.
Though look back, realize,
Things are never going to be the same.
Things are constant.
At war this is.
A future without.
That is my dreamland.
Past lives and memories wounded, salted, and filled with mud,
Will wounds ever heal?
Back to the war at Hitler's main command.

Turn the tides, yes, indeed, you have.
Now bring on the Chaos at Dunkirk
France flees fast from the Germans and
The saviors of the battle where field was woe to fight any more.
Flee was the choice for more than 300,000 troops and thus,
The miracle of Dunkirk.
Though the flood in 1940
With France, Belgium, and the Netherlands
All three nations under similar forces' attacks at once,
Forcing families from homes,
Though what land is mine is yours till the end.
Why is war still around day to day again?
Has our time not taught us well,
That nothing can be gained for good fortune or fertility wielding weapons of destruction.
What we lose in lives, possibilities for more and power.
We are confused believing that power can be taken or gained.
Neither granted can power be rightfully or properly obtained.
Power, like respect, like trust, like faith, value, belief, all are a simple
System of mind over matter and what your personal life actions portrays will.
Bestow upon you what you earn and deserve.

Thus, which is why war is a loss for our fields outside.
The years our crops have endured the air in their ears to the kind of people
Who have no problem brainwashing each other?
To do each other's bad will wishes.
When will we stand together to just join and help or stand aside and call for help.

Money will doom us as well for trees supply so little from our minds but our lives require what our pockets desire.

The more spaces we build the more items dreamt to acquire to fill.
Overwhelmed inside like a hoarder can swallow their own soul.
Through a long life of choices that are merely blindly being made
Over favoriting memories of least importance for the days are now short
And our memories are now our treasures and as such are burdening our lives.

Cry and shout and slam through and sometimes just set the fire to glory.

8 days with civilians help saved Dunkirk.

But displacement camps and as well the eagerness
To get avengement for the shameful actions by their opposing forces,
And now,
Holy War,
Roman Catholic Schools
Pope Pious the twelfth
Would not hand his photo nor propaganda.

Enraged and insulted internally he raged stronger.
His greed for control needed wealth capitalized early.
Faking money with enlisted prisoners
To produce fake British pound to create chaos.
In hopes but not much more than interrupt.

Pure German
Book Burning
Blonde hair blue eyed
Our land's race must be German purified.
Was this Hitler's delusional idealistic.

Perfect child campaign had the wrong effect when an Austrian child was brought up as a Jewish in an attempt to fault.

Charlie Chaplin was an anti-Nazi activist.

Who funded his own "The Great Dictator"?
Charles Limburg runs for president.
What was that again?
Was that the wind?

Take to the skies and bomb them blind!
Was the best idea coming to mind as Britain used?
The downing system to foil the nazis bombers attacks.

C.S. Lewis describes the life of the possibility for children to escape.
As parents would send them to the countryside to escape if they could.
'The Lion, The Witch and The Wardrobe."

Britain was not the best if the air through the war statical stasis,
Edging on 3,700 RAF aircraft with half being high-speed fighter craft.

On the other side was the:

Luftwaffe boosting in their 4,200 aircrafts with over 1,000 of them being fighter crafts,
As well as 1,000 bombers.

But defensive flying and aversive actions are shown to have outheld
For Britain flew high and drove by the fear bombing attackings around and
Skillfully took their shots with precision to supply proficient outcomes.

Tolling in the end was worse for the Germans.

The world does not want to surrender to Hitler.

Hitler went to war on June 22, 1941
German forces invaded the Soviet Union
For the pursuit of race in Operation Barbera Rosa.
Russian land was what was being wasted is how.
Hitler viewed their vast lands with his own dreams
To invade and lay claim for their land as theirs.
All land would be for repopulating and providing.
better use for the self-proclaimed fairer German skin and blood.

Japan attacks Pearl Harbor and retaliations begin against Japan.

Germany and Japan now declare war against the United States

The same day the United States naval forces were weakened.
and war called upon the Attacking Japanese.

Robert M. Noise was the first American soldier to die as a result of a bombing raid.
Iowa native meteorologist in Norway, a year, and a half before Pearl Harbor.

The 45th infantry division had American is from Oklahoma, New Mexico, Colorado, and Arizona.
They wore a uniform of confusion and redesigned to proper align.

Hitler's train named Amerika.
Causing him to need to stay alert.

Liberty Steak and Freedom Fries to cry for help because our words can't seem to end our wars.
Food as the result always provides most comforts.

Gotta have my coke.

Until Hitler may go up in smoke when he dreams to invade Russia and should have listened to Napoléon who learned before him in times past before.

Hard to fight when not on your own turf.

Plotted against by many of his own men.
Executed eighty-four of his own generals as well as many of Hitler's scientists.
Unconventional bug with a Colorado potato beetle causing a nationwide starvation was a line even he wouldn't cross.

Hitler was in World War 1 and had some strange war tactics he had rules for himself.
Bomb development heating in Germany though their uranium may have come into us hands.

And the Canadians now are ahead developing a bomb.

The success of the first bomb, where we have become death, destroyers of worlds,
In the viewers' exact words as seeing it in a New Mexico Dessert.

Fat man and little boy, plutonium versus the forces of uranium-235
With the fat man being 40% more powerful.

William Patrick Stewart, a purple heart soldier whose father was Hitler's brother.

Disease and plague in camps demises many lives, including Anne Frank.

Denmark surrendered to Germany's ways and allowed them to stake claim.
In the mist under their watching eyes,
they snuck all their Jewish community to Neutral Sweden.

Sgt Rodrick Edmonds had taken a huge risk which resulted in potentially saving more than three hundred lives.

The War chant was designed by a Harvard graduate, holding the key to the resemblance.
To the acclaimed college's fight song.

The Soviet Union and Japan were now at war and have been since as there has never been a treaty signing to resolute the times of war ending.

Parachuting Nazi, Rudolf Hetz, atop the Union Building, was arrested, and held a prisoner of war for his crimes.

Brian Donlevy, Orson Welles, Robert Sterling… drafted.

Errol Flynn, Cesar Romeo, and Glenn Ford…
drafted.
Rob Skelton, Dennis Morgan, Robert Taylor…
Drafted.
John Payne, Spencer Tracey, John Wayne and
Mickey Rooney all were drafted.
In the smoke and flames when lives were staked
and news pokes at steaks
Is this world gone in morality and dignity or is
fighting a way of the streets?

I just see leaves that fall into ash and dust just as
the soldiers had done for us.
The tolls of war are the crimes of which we need
to dissolve with minds and words.

Be kind and do not fight in wars.

The Wisdom of an Apple is Threatened by the Confused Greed of THE WORM

A time old tale said: an Apple
a day keeps the Dr. away. Wind
blows worrying past witless Worm
minds just searching for the Tunnel Through
Time.
Look at me just Rambling.
All we need is Happiness.

Desperately, we long for Happiness
which was lost under Apple
tree's back in our fantastical Rambling
minds wishing to bring Wind
with us into journey to Tunnel Through Time.
Have we become the Worm?

Disappeared have the Worms
gone. Long roads ahead if Happiness
is truly desired. Tripping a Tunnel Through
Time
sounds fun? Stick out those Apple
leaves from under your tongue. Wind
blows your sins to Ramblings
of memories in past lives. Rambling
is the lies laid down as a Worm
wiggles itself down- Wind
of any hopes for Happiness.
Rotting; it caused the Apple.
Still hoping for the magical Tunnel Through
Time?

Travel through your minds before trying to
Tunnel Through Time.
Express today correctly. Rambling
is for blank pages. Respect the Apple
that battled the Worm
by holding faith in its own ability to provide
Happiness
after by doing so. Strong Winds

shake trees as gusts of Wind
span endlessly wishing to close the Tunnel
Through Time.
To allow us everlasting Happiness
at last and a night for Rambling

to be left for the Worms
to chatter through; rather than the Apple.

Wrongfully biting the Apple
may spin angry Winds.
Close your mouths. Shhhh….. No more
Rambling.
Have we the right or capacity to Tunnel Through
Time?
Have we learned from the Worms?
Or neigh? Could we safely say a cat was our
teacher in Happiness?
Fin

Fear

Fear is lurking when we hide our shame behind faked smiles that shadow our pained regrets.
Life allows one chance to make the most with the vessel of life we are blessed with to cherish.
Whether life is good or bad is up to the walker to decide each moment as they continue.
Each breath is the journey of a lifetime. Each bat of an eye could be the opening to a new gate.
When we realize our minds will trap us or free us, but we are the key keepers who must control…
Will we have time in the end if we worry away the middle after finally learning from the beginning?

Insanity is continuing to repeat the same action over again with expectation for a different outcome.
Madness can easily consume those over preoccupied.
When I drive down the roads to complete any day task, I see faces that are daily dangerous as their actions reveal the ignorant negligence that a like-minded child or absent-minded wonderer might assume forward.
To indirectly for any reason place any other's life or wellbeing in harm's way will light Karma's pen writing a handwritten doom note to demerit your life's worth in a matter of your own selfishness biting you back one day when it's least expected.

History is meant as a guide to help us learn by example what to avoid going forward.
Rather than this, would our future generation of young minds be better learning the skills and functionalities they will need in their lives to prosper, adapt, flourish, and survive?
If we stand divided, we are a weakened entity.
If we fight while holding grudges blindly in hands, the sweat will tear our fake finger ties to shreds of wasted skin.

Honesty, respect, listening, patience and kindness will pave a path towards unity and dignified morality.
This can not be a forced path to walk as it also will not be an easy nor a short path.

It will be a righteous path of soulful serendipitous glee while exploring virtues and values in all life.
Together we must believe in our planet as one, or none will be prepared for the day we many billion of lives and eyes whose hearts all beat *bump* *bumph Bump* *bumph* *bumhp bumph bumph* *bumph* as the fear keeps our tongues suppressed forcing words the likes of our minds scrambled to keep trapped down our throats to the point our stomachs hurt from faking day in and day out that voice or that smile while you don't even feel the strength to take one more step in that mile to nowhere you keep circling.

OCD is tapping into the linear dimensions of lifetime insanity.
The inability to let go and accept change.
Deterring change from occurring is as negative as obstructing justice.
It disrupts natural peace and serenity if one can not accept as seen fit situationally.

The stakes are high for the last word. The first punch. The final "HAHA". Or the opera concerto performance by the fair lady in the high chambers for her final ensemble where she sings the resonance of tones we merely imagine to be bestowed from the heavens into a cathedral like such majesty.

A daydream… or reality waiting? Calling?
Nothing was ever possible, provable, or realistically achievable until one person focused enough energy to dream the impossible into a functioning possibility.
It all starts somewhere.
It is up to us where the roads truly end.
Almost all of the world's best ideas or inventions were seen as radical or crazy before becoming accepted as a norm.
We choose what we title as crazy.
Why not test the roads or wade the waters before taking the swan dive headfirst?
If we do not teach by our best examples of our own self-image, then what future do we expect to be approaching other than a lonely one with questions of why not's and I wish this or that's.
Do what you can today for what you wish for tomorrow.

Patience brings the most blessed tidings as the wait will surpass true worth for any value by weight.
Time is money and money does grow on trees.
We kill time savouring money and all for more money while lives are wasted.
Hours and minutes tick by all while lowering air supply and love as was intended is merely passed for opportunity to gain as time is not nearly as important when a green bill waves a crinkled wink of persuasion our way.
Mind moves where our masters brainwashed us to follow. Holler louder dollar, we're all struggling to follow.
Monopoly, was that really just a game? It feels as if most of us do not get to pass go and collect two hundred without paying the bank extra to keep us safe first.
Where is the path to follow leading towards a croaking pool of lilies and flies and fish tales wishing silently nearby though unseen to our sights.
Just prove that money doesn't make decisions for our towns.
Promise me people don't stab a life to smithereens for some silly symbol man made us believe is such an importance?
It's a trap laid before any one of us could ever count time.

The passage into the new lands led them not to find gold coins.
King William or whoever when they voyaged found a more invaluable asset even more of interest to trade for its qualities were indicative of a natural found persuasion.
Addiction.
Money is a trap for them once they find what you tick to.
Many turn to drugs.
Many work for love.
Liquor is better than liquid tears.
Price to live life with a smile while society deteriorates soul's better than encourage.

Governed by the pockets wiped clean monthly by maids of maize field.
Corny, pungent and foul beings it must take to find pleasures in ranking over those less experienced.

How did the world turn so Blue?
Turning, turning, everlastingly going.
Does anyone ask Our Planet Blue,
Oh, What Can We Do For You?

For we show no cares for the space our ecosystem spares as our air to be us in.
Believe that what you need, is what we all need.

What the Earth needs as well.

We all need to step back,
Breathe,
Hydrate,
Walk It Out,
Scream or Shout,
Jump All About,
BLINK….. Breathe in… out… in…
Close our eyes, hold that breath,
Breathe all the hate you have ever experienced or passed for any reasons,
Catch it in your gut and spin it round and around festering your entire bloodlines anger boiling into a sputtering glowing emotional hot air fireball in your chest and with all of that focus…
Exhale your breath in a long slow motion allowing the memories to now have no ends to regrow that pain from.
Allow your breath to refresh your lungs and open your mind as you open your eyes to the day as it was, has been and will continue, but with the knowledge that you are in the driver's seat of your destiny and you owe it to yourself to enjoy it rather than to hold on to any times you felt a moment had been wasted.

Far Out

Life, not as complicated as we made it and still make it appear to be. How hard can something be if the word can explain itself. Here we go. Let me spell it out though. The meaning of life is to LIVE! Why was this ever questioned to the point it feels outdated and so under-rated.

There is a star. So, so very afar. To my catalogue it is referred to as "pink star 1136-247" and is so strong that the sun relies on this to exist. So much more relies on this sun. point of explanation be here, not to be made of words unclear. Hear this to all who presently exist.

This star I referred to is an 'energy equalizer suction type system' that takes in all energies that come within reach of the right type. These types are as follows:
Now- don't think too hard on this. It's too simple to complicate.
+ Positive and – Negative
I warn all of life, learn what happiness is. Forget what worries are! Live and Love as you do you. I hope it's not hard to understand that Planet Blue 282-006 creates an influx of terminally ignorant and nontolerant negligent toxic negative energies and it's saddening for me and others I know to see our kind leaving a trail of disrespect and lack of common sense that are now spreading like a virus into our special eco-solarium system. If we can not fix ourselves, then learn to evolve yourselves to fit your silly greedy needs.

Time is as time was.
Life is what you decide for it to be.
Don't ever waste any of your time being in misery.

Leaves array,
Turning more colors
Each and every day.

Sun in the sky,
Wind gusts right on by.
Feeling brisk and chilly upon your face.

If we rely on playing the field, how about we prepare ourselves and the entire area in mind as well. If we can care for our land now- before we continue to lose time and track of place, there could be an extended future more worth it than any box a cat could fit in.

That dab brought flavors and rememberings
Of Skittles and Twizzlers….
Even Sour Patch Kids… yeah.
I can't tell you how, but that dab was like
I took a shower through that smoke toke
Emerging a flower fresh into a field
Growing powers behind rainfalls
Tucked into beautiful rock beholding
Nature sculptures abound supplying
With all sorts of life and green goodness
Growth surrounding. The breeze.
No longer alarming. The air?
Clear and calm. Peace is here,
For at least my head in that moment.

Try this idea on for size too for a toll booth can replace a ticket maid, though our teachers are our best virtues.

To simplify their jobs and provide less risk for all, how about teaching by virtual reality schooling? All necessary sports teams and extracurricular classes can be held during normal hours in more vacant schools.

Talk about calm learning?
Talk about less commute times for all?
Virtual reality education- VRE
With Virtual reality education assessments- VREA

Virtual reality education developer- VRED
Virtual reality education support- VRES
Virtual reality education testers- VRET

Virtual reality education center- VREC
Virtual reality education producer- VREP

As If

As if to say, the book be true. As if time led us to self-divide our own souls, as if to be first meant a glowing key to the universe.
As if asking as ifs didn't really exist. As if we all lived to live.
As if we never spread our legs and eggs so far.
As if roads didn't tear rivers apart.
As if forgiveness was foreseeable in all our hearts. As if just being together could blow away this burst of stormy weather.
As if to live life we stopped the cheating and tuck away our grimaces. As if makeup did change our faces.
As if life was a race and we all woke up late, but it was cancelled due to hail on the boardwalk so big they bounced higher than the doorways.
Here, as if, we weren't still all rushing down the

roads hoping to not have to wait in any extra line.
As if, clown college wasn't what Earth became.
As if, this year of 2023. As if we can agree to disagree.
As if we expect the respect in prioritizing our needs more before we explore our wants.
As if, we all realize we all exist. As if we realize we all started the same exact way.
As if, the question of "Which came first; the chicken or the egg?"
As if we learn that stories have many turns and sides unheard.
As if though my head said that today it must have been the chicken who came when she laid her eggs down.
As if though, to believe, that a chicken enjoys the experience of pushing out those ovals out of their holes.
As if "Holes" taught us more about being resourceful.
As if for 2023, we spend a week for Thanksgiving break.
Literally, shut all work down in the world.
As if, we could prepare for this.
As if we could all relax at this.
As if this dream came to exist.
As if we all had a potluck and passed food around like in "The Grinch" with the "Who's".

As if we no longer cared who's who and we just cared because we see
(You and you, all of us, we make up this life we live on our world together.
As if lending a hand to help wasn't such an outburst of interruption to us.
As if this week of Thanksgiving was celebrated by all and truly appreciated. Pass food, spend time at home.
As if this life improving "finger's crossed" event came to happen, as if we recorded it. As if.
As if we recorded it all, but not live.
As if we spent our days in the town square's state centers we live in or have family in or whatnot.
As if we spent sunup, till sundown embracing positive energies and stories.
As if we all brought something family-sized to provide for each day. Further as if, for if everyone to have enough food on their plate to not leave hungry.
Then to if, as the night shifts, as if we all had free Netflix.
As if, bellies full, we all together watch Netflix and chilled. As if each day all week long, at 4:20, the world smoked the glorious Mary Jane toke.

After as if, as 5 o'clock strums around, we all
raise our beers hoping for much more pleasant
of years forward to come.
As if we all saw ourselves as babies and seniors.
Students and teachers. Leaders and followers.
As if we all walked our own path and as if we
breathed to see no pain hiding or splattering our
streets.
As if Pangea wasn't thunderstruck and plates
collapsed and misplaced some flaps.
As if life wasn't worrying if you have a muffin
top. As if though, we worry if we are happy?
As if we question our own actions before others.
As if we hold our judgments to ourselves.
As if our criticisms led us to cat-villa of
curiosities and we investigated our ideas of
unknown.
As if, to this day and age.
As if we now are regularly living to see older
ages.
As if our heartbeats helped us walking each day
in the streets.
As if. Anger. Jealousy. Hate.
As if these were a concept in our mind.
As if more. Going back in time. We were linked
to species and bodies of man-wo-man who
seemed to survive off the land as best they could
see fit.

As if, we now realize true survival of the fittest.
As if we stopped worrying if it's going to get us.
As if we took death as a grace for the life these souls lived, now gone. Our soul's journey continues.
As if we simply opened our hearts to more than our mind allows our eyes to see or our ears to hear.
Listen with your heart.
Hardly imagine where the world could be today, if hundreds of years ago at first signs of spite in rage, if those emotions were nipped like a quick spit on a traveling ember from a roaring fire pit.
Extinguish the bad and the good can fill the lack we near desperately crave to feel whole.
We equalize ourselves when we do just that.
This was the goal ever since we declared ourselves to be divided and separate.
The wars will have no end. The story will not be happy to read to the last page at our rate.
All we need is a little respect when we come home.
All we need is to grasp the if's and make them when's.
Once our dreams become thoughts, they fester and develop into our words or actions.
The more this follows suit, the sooner any change will be noticeable and encourage more.

Nothing gets better when things are at their worst. Things need to just get a little better for a revolution to take place.
No human can roam the world alone by foot. What is possible is if the world roamed together in support for our best chance in survival which is strength in numbers.
When we stand divided, we fall and crumble away like the cookie crumbs that monster leaves chasing and Hansel and Gretel resort to for final hopes of survival, yet rather, doom follows these crumbs.
Though alone we stand tall, but seclusion is no easy answer for all. To the loneliness is a slow mind collapsing doom for resources and knowledge of insights or advice need to come from another's eyes for our wings can never spread for a mere human to have multiple viewed perceptions from the beginning.
Leaving the answer to the last space, as the best is so often saved for last. End the competition. We have together to hold true and to group our spirits when hopes to feel low.
Together we strive to be the most effortlessly coexisting and evolving species as of our knowledge yet.

In a World

In a world where our each and every turn,
We often forget to question whose to gain or lose
From each action we make or choose.

So, for many hunger is a norm,
As awful for them to know,
That tables nearby are wasting bits
And whole carcasses just for safety's sake.

Being fair is not easy when all our lives
Life is always at war.

This is what makes us stronger
If we look into how to develop bonds better.

People are a race of species.
Benevolent and mysterious as far

Superior and inferior.

Opposites that attract also tear our inner seams.

When we remember the trickling tone of a stream,
Or the guitar strum or beat down on a drum.
What makes the world happy is when we all have our space.

Space is vast and wide, and circles or squares cannot hide.

What can be hidden is self.
Thus, the meaning of selfish and selfless.

To be one and to be the other is both one and the same.

To be a helping and caring being is to be one who lives to be the best self they can see for the world around them to be at least disturbance and most hope for peace.

This is the way we wish to spread sweet dreams.
Is it not?

I can not imagine a world where:
If there are no hungry bellies at night;

If there is no jealousy or reason to fight.
If there was no need to hurt another.
More.
No worries of wars.
No worries to open your doors.
No worries of being forced to fight fights you didn't start.
Reasons for answers.

To believe in a time where all division of man and woman.
Or adult or child.

Of any person near or far.
If we open our knowledge from the past as a new way to a better tomorrow.

Is this an action I would approve of for today's people?

Yes. As I as well have questions from past views and reports that we may all wish answers found in our research.

As one must ask though.
The day-old question.

If answers were laid on the table, clear as can be and no other choice can change what may be done;

Will just the peace of knowing the truth provide these same sweet dreams we may need?

Can closure be as closed as a book, and we hold no more anger or spread no more hate from just knowing may end our hearts' ache?

At the end of the road, as we reach a bench near the bend of the tree-encased lake with wind pushing crinkled leaves about the frosty summer air.

Reminiscent of the sunrises and sorrowful of lost sunsets as we often miss and lose those from interest.

Better issues need to be in mind when any one further goes to government or public time.

We hurt so many lives by “trying to teach them of their crimes;”
But really it should be more like:
“Hey, I’ll make more money off you are being in prison and ruin your life forever so your dime is a never-ending dollar fill up.”

It's sad when lives are so clearly at such a loss for words that fakeness and rage or mistaken glances can end all further breaths or dancing chances.

Leftovers and sleepovers. Tumbleweeds and dancing trees.

Horseback by the beach and a sudden stunning red fox running down the street.

Don't forget to smell the daisies and look around some more so you don't go crazy.

Love each step or you may make a big regret.

Life is more than dollar bills and a true smile will fill your pocket more and a hug can fill your house with bountiful warmth.

Blood is thicker than water.

Which is why I finally believe I understand the reason why Jesus may have made a metaphor in his action of turning said "Water into wine."

How divine would it be to say all of time that family holds us together?

As well that blood is thicker than water.
But the grapes of wraith they fill with ash
When water turns to wine.
Of family a bickering,
And time keeps flickering.
I wish to live with mere merriment
And let go of distribuend.

And so, the message I translate as I see it is that wine, may poison us.
And so may water.
It's all in the battle and knowing when to choose which for when you need to win or lose.

The cat's up on cloud nine are the ones whose bellies are almost never hungry for their whiskers would soon turn to mush or jelly.

Smell the flowers some extra before you take your next bend.
Catch your own fish to fry as a Sunday surprise.

The time you spend will only make you as happy as you equivalate the probability of happiness out to be.

Thus, is how the simplest things in life are often just undeniably the greatest.

Like a giant steaming fresh plate of
home-cooked perfectly fluffy and moist cracked
with pure and tender love and care.
Yes! Scrambled eggs of course!
And the best side to any plate of eggs, besides
some cheese on top,
Is a whole pile of bacon nearby.
And whoever doesn't just love popping their
bacon into their microwave for sheer
convenience and easy bacon pleasure: You're
straight lying to yourself in my eyes.
But a home-cooked meal can brighten any mood
and lift about any negative spirit.

So stars will always seem bright when the night
has gone darkest.
And the sun rise will always rise from the east
and west to its sleep.

And the 365.25 days our revolving ball of blue
and brown and green gloop takes to make
another full cycle;
All with a whole other group of planets and
other eco and solar systems known and unknown
so far to exist.

What a crazy and beautiful gift we all have of
life on this planet.

Are we going to waste one more second fighting or wasting time, resources, energy, or money? For what reason? Pride? Respect? Bragging rights?
I want to brag when we are all in a state of time when no one around the planet is struggling. When no where is there any more hatred being spread by past negligent parties' actions. Turning the keys to each person's destiny is not easy and not every one will always fulfill their destiny.

We make our life how we can and not every step is up to our control.
As well, many other factors take a toll or help our growth in our time from embryo, to infancy, child, adolescent, young adult, middle-aged, golden-aged and finally elderly.

There is no set span that all these stages of life will line up for along any group of people.

Therefore the best we can really do, and are doing, is making charts. Taking data.
With most accurate and detailed information, the graphs could show a whole new blend of pie we may not ever have realized was possible but was in the oven the whole time.

Who truly knows who searches endlessly for the answers of which their questions do lead them towards?

Follow the yellow brick road?
Red pill or blue pill?
Did you see where that rabbit went?

All time and time was will ever more be merely a memory.
Life is and isn't as it seems; why else would so many question if it were all just a dream?
DOROTHY! DOROTHY! Just keep Toto locked up and we'll all be alright.

Poetry of One Words

The real problem I see continuing to prosper is
the draining adventure in our souls.
The only thing that is holding us down is the end
of the road and not knowing where it goes.
The paths we are now all are following are led
by our phones as no maps are told to scroll for
us.
The fates of minds have twisted our hearts and
darkened our thoughts as a world of sad folk.

A pen writing the stage is suddenly overtaken
and the words make no sense, confusion is
consumed.
The feeling is odd, and the fear is leaving as
everything fades and my body is soothing away.
The flip of a narcotic that melts away the worry
into nothing.

This action of adding the ability to release is devastating too much.

Truthfully, we have a necessity to feel the bad that we wish to hide however we can find.
Filling a hole or void temporarily with a substance to cover the feelings is a sham.
For what is a sensation if we have no experience to relate them to compare?

Any injury could all have been the same if we had a magic fix.
All our sufferings could free from our minds and the harm held within steps away out of our body.

To hear and believe in living carefully,
After understanding the sorrows of having no mornings tomorrow if daily spent careless.
Fulfilling purpose and voyage through is spelling care in every step like walking on wondrous thunder.

To the ones who need it most, the drugs fit the bill for the love they lost in living their life.
Pain is a powerful fringing feeling that we want to dispose of as soon as it succumbs.
Make sure to go with the flow for addiction will bite you when you flee and break down yourself.

Remembering memories and wishing to relive
the same or differently.
Though one thing that will remain is that time is
definite and what is, was and will have always
been.

Changing is as hard to accept as is to choose
who or what to love as true to cherish each day.
A movie or a song can be paused, reversed, and
rewind a VHS but the steps we take are one to
relish in.
Each opportunity we have is ours to take it or
pass as we make millions of minute decisions
daily.
What is the point of life? Why are we alive?
Aging questions that the answer is only up to us
now.

Take each day as the gift it is for before we
know the wrinkles grow over our eyes and the
time flew fast.
Our mind is telling us to act our age when what
does that mean?
The test to pass to obtain a license to drive
seems it may have simplified.
Where is home when the roads are never alone
as now, we are left wandering the streets meek.

To a swimmer, a dive is a refreshing idea. To another it may be a terrifying concept to imagine.
The regrets we should realize before it is ever too late is the concept of ignorance in society.
Do that tomorrow is what a slacker says. Take the chance that it could be lack of knowledge.

Lose yourself in the stars if your heart loses feeling purpose any longer.
The knowledge of love and the power of family and support.
Follow the roads that lead you to those energies in the most positive force.
Taking every opportunity to discover the lost and open road may lead to the best paths.

So often the stories shared by children who, now as adults, understand why they hated growing up.
The equation to compare is of reliant input pointing to family being an invaluable aspect needed.
Teachers in school are one of the most helpful role models as a child learns and gains skills.
Classes offer options for creativity to begin to flourish like music, art, sports, or theater.

Social skills are attributed to developing early
and the voice then grows strength to talk among
friends.

As we grow wiser, minds are taunted by the
cravings bestowed for the tasty beers that
beckon.
When the best-selling book of all time is
beckoning a story of a man turning water to
wine,
And other religions put faith in the cow that our
land slaughters to build beefy burgers.
Our French fries are so highly acclaimed that the
catastrophes can change our freedom when
squished.

Our land that we lay our lives in upon ending
breathing, could be a growing farm of
nourishment.
Where our best workers of all time, yes, the
horses, can roam and aid with all duties needed.
Where all sheep of any color are nurtured the
same and none are left to rot alone or cold.

Beside the bedside and under a full-lit moon is
where the sparkles of the night send calm rays
out.
However long we enjoy a flavor is up to our
tastes together to bud and bottom within.

Watching what we consume for a disease lurking in delicious bites could lead to a fatal tomb.

Forever though, to live and waste as leaching upon the lowest streets you can face to walk.
When a mother births a baby from their womb, a chance is taken in her life as well.
To wish that one does not exist is to be an ungrateful soul and to change your view is to you.
The deal will never appeal to a fish when believing they are always out of water walking in gravity.

To the day we have and the value that was bestowed but we have way to influence.
If we gave way to our voice being a positive energy just daily. Just daily. Be positive. Try.
The morning is the best place to start. If that be "midnight oh one" as first morning sign, what have you.
One word of advice is to turn away from abuse altogether. Be the one who gives hope to the weak.

We all feel confused occasionally. When losing faith in where to go, do not venture alone.
Together the odds will be stronger if minds are both in full focus.

To say goodbye to the one you love is a gift. To take that gift away by own doings hurts and never fades.
Silent night goes dark as every candle ever lit now memorializes the soul, we wish we knew was pained.

The letters we could write would fill pages with dropped tears smudging the words never spoken.
And angel whose time leaves upon own mind and takes time in one day to a stop suddenly.
All indoors now fall as your well-rounded attempt with each step and breath goes by.
In the lasting blink from your eyes watching freedom around feeling fleeting.
Oh, to the removing of bad feelings. Oh, to cover up for pains we wish to flee from us.

No trauma will compare to what there is when there is nothing left to compare.
Acting daily ourselves with makeup plastered faces is foreshadowing the gentility of personality inside.
No grievances can be ensured if acting as yourself, you are not true to your real self.
Place down the tools you are building your walls before you lose yourself in your boxed wall prison.

Any crack can mend or continue. Following
forward is nerve aching to crumbling down.
The true heroin is the one who frees themselves
from heroine and its nasty clutches.
Drugs tolling the goods lost to the gates of
Heaven would now fill too many vans to
imagine in view.
Why is a needle a cure and a curse? Why can it
help and harm, heal and hurt? Conundrum.

A pen as well has multiple types and in medicine
world can save or kill us as well.
When the plan though, has stages for any
outcome that could ensue, protection is nice.
We can win with our minds and if once we saw
and joined minds rather than rage war.

There will never be happiness when we cannot
freely walk or dance in our yard or streets.
Then again, many are too ignorant or negligent
to understand or have any empathy to care.
The dream that was once dreamed, is losing
strength in what was a shout, now seems
whispering.
Holding on tight to the hopes the glass will refill
if any combustion is consumed.

Reliving hurt is a journey of fools for the relief
comes from better times ahead.

Each time we give energy to view past times when pain was strongest, is wasting possibilities now.
Our mind can be a tool to build us up or break us down.
Our heart can be a source of support as well as the strongest force to break our spirits.

The most common connection is when teardrops all are shared in a moment of silence in the rain.
Free the anger trapped in our boots to the tips of our gloves.
Mellow the sadness as if it were the sand sweeping away from your skin in the sun-kissed wind.
Feel free to live in joy and be aware of fear while allowing yourself the control.

Resentfully living is a waste and realizing thus will only open doors.
If a world worries alone, all behind closed doors, can it be forced to come to a spiraling end?
A reflection is mirrored by an opposite view and a composite view is perceived.
Wind could whisper a leaf to another state as we could embody our forces to be true as gold.

If our direction was for fate to entail, then where is our belief in mystery?

If rain fell the same every time and the weather
was predictable, why wonder anymore?
To be fulfilled is to fill each day with journey
and question as much as desired.

Do you want to kick the bucket ever while in a
KFC establishment? I would rather not.
Summarize to the ecstasy of bliss that leads
drooping downward to an everlasting spiral.
When an epiphany feels it would be an effortless
vital ease and it must go viral.
Well, when I ask, will society wonder if what
they tick tock away day to day has any worth?

Our lives have run dry. As a gas tank in a
pristine classic car that drove to our time in a
bubble.
Gasp. Laws of all time and space negate this.
But if. These cars and a driver came to our time.
I can envision the frozen expression as their jaw
drops as their gas runs dry and the prices sky
high.
A spoon is plunged deep into the working-class
pockets that support the upper class.

Intention to do right and doing so are entirely
different concepts and aspects.
Too soon another is taken by force, or pressure.
You who do it, carry the heaviest guilt overall.

As elders, often we wonder why any younger are chosen to leave this planet so young.
Doom will take our breath one carcass at a time, and the harder we worry, the faster we ring.
The graveyard attendant listens when we least desire him to. When our cries are loud and sorrowful.

Each opportunity we have in life we have an adventure and take this as an advantage to live.
The end is not where our worries should lie for this will only shorten our story. Unexpected can happen.
One person only paves the path. Walk route A to B. Make sure to make it your own.
If our desires and songs of wishes are cross twisted, then yes, hell will appear the life we live.

Earth is overtaken if we allow such to happen.
We can only learn from history if we look for the lesson.
We find an error and we take the eraser to hide the shame. There is no soothing to losing vanity.
What a narcotic does is embellish the negative.
Pride is gone when pushing away closes doors.
Beauty is added endlessly when the effort is effortless. Genuine and original shine brightest.

Never mind the belief of clarity viewing another's desired necessity. Assumptions of ignorance.
To know the calls from one substance to said user, is a sham to claim and an instant mistrust placed.
Alone is a sensation of strong amplitudes. Precisely why boredom and solitude arise from madness.
Injury is often difficult to recover from and alone odds are worse than with supplied support.

Suffering within is worst when fear is strong just asking for help, though desperately needed.
How much more careful can one who is accident prone to be and still be followed by mistakes.
If living life is a struggle, then the hill we face may be most due to carelessness.
To cherish this body, soul, and time, care for yourself and all else around as well and all should be good.

When It Comes to Depression

When it comes to depression
Here's a little story
All about a young girl
Always aiming for glory.

Nothing eternally.
Just hopes for equality.

Dreams crushed by the plows
Clearing the way to eventually feed us to the cows.

Who cares what happened who knows when to who knows who.

Did it happen to you?
If you said no then leave that page in the past.

His Story can be told in a flash that there's really hardly a purpose to reminiscing back.

Looking forward to seeing you,
Living each day for the world to one day sit beside us.
Why couldn't we put grudges in stones and drink away the memories of any thrones.

Paving the new roads for unforeseen destinies to unfold.

Hey hey, I know I'll be okay.
It's just another one day,
Maybe it'll get better by Sunday,
Please tell me it'll be okay, okay,
Someday, Sunday, Okay, Hey hey.

I just wanted to say I'm okay,
Though I feel like I was used like your ashtray.
Though I never meant to feel unspoken,
And now I'm left here to feel broken.
How do I not destroy my today,
When I'm always stuck in yesterday.

Hey hey, I know I'll be okay.

It’s just another one day,
Maybe it’ll get better by Sunday,
Please tell me it’ll be okay, okay,
Someday, Sunday, Okay, Hey hey

Whisker's Whippin

There once was a cat, he was very loud, furry, and fat. A real cookie and cream Oreo, For his fur looked black but was the darkest of browns.

He was dark with glistening white mixed in. The best was the milk moustache
That spread from his top lip to spread down to the
Lower side as if it ran down like milk stached.

This cat was fast to think
For his needs were important to meet in a flash.
His meow echoes far and wide
If he feels in his whisker as if he's being ignored.

"WHY won't you look at me?
I'm hungry mommy!!!
Pet me! Pet me! Pet me now! Wait, not there."

The demands for love are flowing
For chosen you are as the one I trust.
Don't let me down and I will never leave you
cold.
My nose will nudge you mommy when you
sleep,
And my extra fur will comfort your tired feet.
I love you for staying with me,
Even when I keep meowing and you can hardly
Seem to figure out that for which I am wishing.

Meows I spread and fish you lay in a dish for
me.
Cute walks I do and twirls lead me to earn
A whole new world as you trick me to
Supply my treats as eggies in a way to feed my
Kitty craving's needs.

Temptations and treats are what you shake as my
Four legs chase that bag at every opening.

I love the smells, the sounds, and the crunches
When these snacks come down to my delight.
As well as when my mommy knows
Just how I prefer my water to flow.
She's so good to me that she even spoils me
As she provides my water from a fountain.
In my dreams I run and meow with joy.
Giving out chirps as I chase at birds.
I even wonder mountains and meet my mom
Beside my pop and my brother louie two.
Before chasing my dreams to waking with
meows.

My fur is filthy as every single petting session ends with clustering bushels of me flowing through the house in the air current. It drives my dad and mom crazy, yet they have a machine that sucks it up.

It is almost as if my happiness shines from my purrs inside to greet your lips as they start to turn upside and as your smile grows, yes, my tummy may have grown as well. We are best well rounded, right?

The importance is me and my brother kitty. Now my mommy sees that we both need and love each other.
Never separate kitty a from kitty b for they do create Ying and Yang together.

Happy kitty,

Fat kitty,

So soft and full of fish.

Hippy kitty,

Fast kitty,

So addicted to his catnips.

Smelly kitty,

Fuzzy kitty,

Litter boxes are nice,

though baths still hated yearly.

Kitty beats his heart aloud with every single meow.
His night is never dark,
Even with night vision,
His heart is always full as well as his belly.

Whiskey Francisco and Louis Tedstone.
Brothers from separate litters who are smart together.
Kittens who know that love binds, food nourishes hungry minds and the little footsteps.
Though nothing makes our day song brighter than when our mommy chirps those magic words:
"EGGIES! Who wants some Eggies?!"

Those four legged creatures know the bag, the wood of the floor around the area, The sound of each cabinet near their bags' location and who else can smell the crunch from their sleep than one of these two hungry, hungry kitties.

The temptations are a fancy treat that brings us running fast to feast. Kitty a and kitty b are always close in time and space to eat.

Four legs running as they remain our best friends.
Best Furrends until the very end. Meows.

_________________FISH_______________

Suggestions for a Wall to Fall

I suggest a strike.

I suggest this for the current times have gone too far.

No person should be forced to work multiple jobs to SURVIVE.

I CALL FOR STRIKE!

Strike down your timetables and listen hear loud and clear.

Take a stand to the big bosses who floss their asses with bills washed in our faces.

The shower time is near.

Bring the world to a day more clear.

Nonsense I see on a daily.

Common sense fleeing minds more easy.

Time to toss the towel.
Time to relax while the grovel.

Is this world going to survive if we continue in our state of mass confusion?

I rarely see this as a bright or pleasant paved destiny.

Times too hard. Slaves to the pay day.

How hard are you working to live?

Does work let you live?

Can you feed yourself and practice self-care?

Do you have the ability to supply your own piece of mind in a slice of warm mind pie?

Let me ask, for a strike again.

The top companies need to respect that all have an equal deserving of a proper opportunity to plain and simply…
Survive.

The rules many live by and struggle through the torture,
Current generations lost many lessons.
What I extend is a prayer of hope.

A light of sunshine to ray through more clouded mind and roll the crown down the hill to disperse worth to all the towns folks.

Time is of only value.

Only thing irreplaceable on earth is time.

Tell me a plate broke. May have had meaning to you. Or whoever.

But any object, man made or natural in formation, all is there and will remain in some state.

But the lives we lead, the strides we make.

These affect life besides us each day.

Strike the pages.

Ring the bells.

Live now for yourself without neglecting or
dispersing personal negative energies to
environment contained around ourselves as well.

Let me hear loud and clear that change is
coming fine and near.

Time is needed. Hear the calls.
Stop aimlessly passing time wandering dead end
halls.

Write clear and sing loud.
Time be now.
Strike for peace and equalities.

New days need new laws and abide we must all.

Lessen the restrictions but simply put and fair
for all.

If we need each other,
Which whether we like it or not,
We need each other.

The world will not survive if we all hold our
hates inside.

I ask and I plead
Hear these words from me.

Thanksgiving to remember I hope to be the end
of strikes.

The time to relax.
To commemorate the new rights.

A job fills time that supplies all needs to survive
on and leaves no struggles if you commit to that
job's shift.

Dedication shows true motivation.

Let me ask again for a calm time
To strike and leave work to work on themselves
Before any more workers are forced to exhaust
themselves.

Through this strike, I advise. Stay safe at home
and work on your throne.

Remember who you are and that's all you need
to be.

The best versions of ourselves are the ones when we can stop hiding or speaking in lost tongue.

May we need not even speak at all.

Silence is the sound that carries peace around the world.

I tell this in mind for to open hearts and spare lost time.

Thanksgiving to remember.

A week long event to record for viewing only when fully enjoyed and past it has become.

But a community, world wide.

This even more than a pilgrimage
Or even a statement of remembrance.

Just merely a time we all should use in which
To unwind for a week.
To celebrate the breaths we took this year and
Mourn for those lives lost this year.

And all years past as well.

To spend the week with loved ones and opening hearts and eyes to those we may normally idly walk by.

Sharing and share cometh back to you.

Which side of Karma's face is the one in which you will be faced to meet one day?

I hope a strike can change the flow.
And create more positive thoughts and actions
Even to the road.

Breathing we must focus on more.
Why oh why is there always such a rush?
I tell you not ignorantly,
But many are slaves to the currency.

Not by choice, and no option to speak out with their voice.

But let me be the one for all to say that an end has to come for otherwise, we blind ourselves to what we have become and what we will create down the road in time to come.

Another thing to share I have for you,
Is time is relative while having correlation.

Disruption in auricle leaving us wondering if
what we understood was even audible?

Thanks to the telephone, we have knowledge at
the tip of a finger.

Reminder to the game we may have played as
kids called exactly this:
Telephone.

Memories anyone?
I remember to play this was a shame
For sitting in a circle we would
As a group of 6-infinite
We would start at one end and pass one phrase
that one whispers to the ear of the person to one
side.

Continues until all the way around the group
And when the phrase is explained for the last
person who heard, and to recollect as well
through
Backpacking backward through the circle, often,
as it seems, the original sentence was lost and
gone after maybe 3-4 people had to repeat after
hearing once and interrupting what they heard to
verbalize again into eligible words.

So sticks and stones,

Place them down.

Words and hearts
Fill with sparks.

Remember not,
Fight or flight.

Try instead
To converse it or disperse it.
Walk away if truly nothing nice you have to say.

And again, strike one for the pages and relax for real.
Time is longer lasting when you're younger because your body has more flexibility to remain stronger.

So live while you're young because the golden ages in years spanned in time is not gold because our bodies are prime, but wise have we or do we hope to have become by the time golden years spray wave to our fears.

Thanksgiving to remember that we need strength in positive numbers.

Spread the love and end ignorance and negligence.

Take control of yourself and change what needs to be changed.

Don't accept anything you are not happy with for it makes you struggle.

But do not pass your struggles to make others have to struggle for you.

Be kind and kindness will often follow.

Expect nothing while giving it your all.

Thank you and

WELCOME TO FALL!!
Happy Autumn 🍁

Vaccination Fade

Take it easy now y'all.
It's okay to breathe for a moment.

Remember, caring for others starts with our own self-care.

You can't show gratitude, respect or appreciation if you haven't already accepted yourself for your true worth and accepting as well your own faults.

Perfection is the realist lie we could ever hope for out of life.

Don't try to be perfect.
Come original.
Be you.
That's all you were designed to do.

Try instead to desire only happiness.

Try more relying on practice and lessons learned.

Teaching more through your own journey rather than forcing the words you're told to be implementing.

Does it matter if nothing else has?

We will never change while we are said to be comfortable.

World was designed for change. And we have become stagnant in terms of development in Human Resources along the proper ethics and morality line.

Please, hope for the life you dream to wake up to live.

Be the person you want to meet on the street.

Be the one that brightens a life, a day, a moment with just a simple phrase of kindness.

Genuineness is a lacking trait.

How much trash has the makeup industry sold to all of us while we hide behind the foundation that we caked on?

Cookies crumbling down now.
And that pie is in the sky.

My life, a la mode.

For no where do I daily see humans even attempting their own self-control.

Me first down the road.

Me most important said the toad to the stool wishing for a good meal.

How lost in time has the golden rule become?

Does this planet have any sense of interest in being truly different?

We have the ability to cook our food. The one main thing in all of time that sets us apart from every species known to humans at this time.

We changed the world when cavemen became comfortable with fire to invent the pit they smoked their first meat steak over.

I don't expect we lay down and roll over.

Our graves are not all yet laid.

Leave memories now in the space of yesterday.

Live breathing for what we know not of which paves our paths ahead.

But enjoy not the curves. The winds and the turns.

We only learn through struggles.

We only overcome when times get tough.

Life isn't meant to be this rough.

We are now so many and we care not to extend that arm of help or that phrase of thanks.

We lucked out in life by being blessed.

We have life still, so chances still there.

Explore more and more and continue opening those doors.

Wished by me, maybe more.

But currently, and coincidentally,
Currency is the most EVIL
Entity I have come to know
To exist to control.

A dime to twirl.
The shiny pearl.
A stagnant piece.
Still though,
A price we carry only in
The minds of the sheep
as they attempt to fall to sleep.

Today, for tomorrow.

For the chance we deserve to not have to ask to borrow.

To take the lies and bar them from our lives.

To turn the radio and news into community filled views.

To take the deception and corruption.

Overrule the unjust and neglect judgement.

We needed a nation to celebrate in hand.

Please, share this hope for a day.
A day ahead with a plan to stop.

Put an end to the hypocrisy of which has become
this of our current society.

I wish, to live equally.
What does that even mean??

To me, to be equal,

Just means to have the same chance to walk the
streets and be happy.

To know I could see a doctor and be helped with
no person to person judgments made that could
have a say on my treatment plan.

We don't want to accept that in time, we have
been lied to.

A general visit from the keepers of the gates
who 1%,

Mainly to say, a slight few have the control slipping from their butterfingers down through the lobbies and to the rules that regulate every single step or breath we are allowed to take.

When in time has anyone ever had to pay a fee to their state, for being employed but unvaccinated?

What world do we live in that now, we have no rights to our own choices of our minds?

Have we as adults been diapered officially?

Have our choices and opinions
And the right to decide how to live
Our own lives as it is our birth right?

The right to decide for yourself,
If you are responsible and respectful
In your personal actions,
Then what is the final debate?

If the vaccine does nothing to the contagious virus,
But will only progress the symptoms to assist my fight for recovery

To me, it's just hard to believe.

To me, it's just hard to trust what they feed me.

To me, is it just me?

To me, I have the right to my body and my soul.

To me, you can't force me to stab that needle into my vein to puppet me the only way you can now.

Scared I am.

The virus claims.

I know nothing of the medical party's shameful and potentially deceitful games.

I want this world to rejoice and breathe again.

Isn't it time for us to all take it easy?

Thank you for the time if any one truly reads each line.

Weighted

Lonely it is. So lonely fear is.
Weighted down
From a young age.
The rolls piled higher
As the muscles grew ever larger.

Strong will and bones
Running on grass, jumping and gasping.
Sports, movement, flexible as tight
Though the weight was still adding on.

Not diet or life had the time
To explain why the body felt tricked.
I slipped. I fell.
The higher they are, the harder they fall.

Truth.
Pain comes barreling down as pounds
Repeat to smash against the ground.

Enemies are feelings and friends we can't miss
For no one sits next to ones they fear might eat
them.

Two hundred before high school for a girl,
Well, instantly uncool I guarantee.

Speech was not a strength for ears betrayed my
head
As just a little baby the words regular to others,
Muddled through my ears. Lost through the
translation.

Much of years I spend in frustration still.
Wondering if my ears stabbed me in my back.
Or was the knife already there when I was born?

It could be just that as I came into this world,
Crushed society of angry eyes.
Many lived lives that were tainted with lies.

Plastered faces of generations when torment was
a normality.
If the judgements were from the grave, then,

Could today be lived for our own to decide in
mind?

But neither was an option really when no chance
to gain
Practice or experience in the general nature of
conversating.

Most of my conversations were with the
cookbooks and mixing bowls.
I have most confidence talking to myself.

Saying things like this might instantly make
others see me as insane
Though if you really;
If you even really knew the extent that I have
endured for pain.

Those muffins I baked for smiles,
Those cakes I brought to class for any reason to
share,
Those cookies I worked to create my own secret
recipe for others to cherish and enjoy as much as
I thoroughly do,
Maybe,
But maybe then we could actually have a
conversation.

Any who judged me without speaking a word,

As this should go to all who judge without first asking of anything,
Ignorant.

Wishing food was a need that we had an impassible limit of intake
That our body comes naturally intact to listen to and so abide by.

Using the oven as a toddler, thankful for a top and bottom set.
Still, needing a tiny step stool to assist my parents.

I knew I was having trouble.
Not much reasons did I have for why.

I knew at night, snacking past midnight.
That gremlin did turn hangry into pure evil energy.

Even if my sleep was not accomplished after that comforting meal,
Then maybe, my dreams were the nightmares of which I troubled most to escape.

For the words most held back in day, or haunted my ears by distance,

They crawled and clambered up my sheets as I
lay,
Helplessly passed fast asleep.

The food helped console the pain that confused
and tore at my inner seams.

Hard as I tried to make and keep friends,
Vanishing faster than the pan of eggs and cheese
or any crispy bacon could fly by,
That's the simple short story of my luck with
talking to people.

I got so tormented over my heavy exterior,
That after living healthy and doing an abundance
of extra activities,
My life had not turned kind to me.

Switched back and forth in high school three
times.
Considered boarding school out of state to avoid
further torture.
I knew my weight was a bolder, but I was not
about to run
Away from my problems to schooling over the
border.

As I was a loner for my age, I did get along great
with those who were elders.

The respect I showed proved that I held no feelings towards others
For I knew the pain of other judgements and I had such wished not to further pass this.

To the extent that a bird can tell a story to mend your pain,
As to, a pizza or a burger so topped would bring me delight.
Never would I have guessed that doom, once again,
Was not at my doorstep.
As not even a junior I wound up meeting the devil.

Abused, trapped, held down as how could I run away when my breath would be gone after a four-step stair walk into my own house?
If you understood through this fat girl's views.
If you were called twinkie though you never once had ever eaten a twinkie.
If you were called a hippo from a seventh-grade girl you had never spoken to before today's class,
Man, those kids; cruel, vile and rude will leave others relentlessly hopeless inside.

If image were no suggestion to a person's nature of being.
It shouldn't be in my mind. But who am I other than a spare tire to be dragged along.

Again, that devil had me trapped. Just like Patrick Star lived in his rock, my weight,
Now adding to the tolls of my decaying life in my dying abusive relationship.
It was all too close to my life being lost.

I was never able to get drunk when I weighed so much.
I was never able to feel anything I felt I should for the main things I felt were inner interference.

The slow tugging of my skin flaps, the dragging and chaffing of my thighs.
When I was young, only 8, I went to Universal with my family,
After a hot day in the sun, the water from the ride was eating my rubbing legs alive.

"DOH" was what my booty read as we walked out of the gift shop in my desperation to hide my legs.
I pleaded to get something to hide and wear to ease the rest of the walk in my wet bathing suit.

Already covering myself with my towel clutched
around me as well as ashamed I was before my
legs.

Why though is something I asked my whole life.
Why to not only the continuous weight pilling
me outwards wider and squarer.
My face swelling like a pumpkin.
My feet like steaks.
Laughed and poked at for having big feet in
school.

Need I also mention that a 13 year old two
hundred pound girl, well, my bits were full
grown.
I had triple D's by the end of 9th grade.
I had my soul give up in high school after
experiencing traumas too close for anyone,
Especially someone who felt alone with no real
words ever to be spoken to offer her comfort.

What trauma did was worsened when doctors
diagnosed what may be a fatal condition.
No even by the condition but by the stigma
attached to it as well.
Never would this chunk be offered help at free
will.
A baby ruth can ease the vain society we enable
to remain a shamble of broken people.

It did not ease my pain for sexual abuse as well as losing the only few I had in my life by my side.
The relationship had turned worse when the devil gave up alcohol for it drove his anger wild.
Though the alcohol made me feel safer in the sense I could get in my car and get away easier.
Though never out the door would I make it for speed the thin stick had over me.

Angered I grew at my weight now stopping me from being freed from my own hell I vowed to stand by.
Before I could think a minute more, as I was returning from my therapist the morning after valentines,
Now only a fifteen minute drive and I had almost ended up losing my life.

Upon waking alone in the hospital,
Never being granted any memory of the accident.
I hit head on 55 to 55.
And not one person lost their life.

A year to decide if I would rot in jail.
Sweet as I could ever care to be, and one wrong move can still end it all.

The days went well and recovered fine.
For a while it was smooth.
The wheels now turning,
Not grinding where they now seemed greased.

A conspiracy I had myself if my own partner
could have called a hit.
For hate had always been filled in his eyes.

I knew that I had to regain myself.
And to a new self-journey I would begin
Of now righting my time I almost lost to the
wind.

I needed to be healthy.
I needed to breathe.
I needed to find a reason to even wake each new
day.

Current times led stress tolls to raise tension.
Never spent a day in detention.
What was my lesson?
Food was the problem. No sugar fix will be a
key to any good opportunities.

I knew the real issue was me.
Was my ability to control my own indications of
how I had self-medicated my pains away.

Silence is my old friend. Food never talked back.
Until it shouts out the back like a wise crack.

Nevertheless, there were little times that compare to the hours I spent in the kitchen learning my skill.

The doctors said, and this a year after I had almost lost my life,
I now had heard I would be lucky to live another ten years if I was unable to change my own habits.

I tried my whole life to eat right. Though I ate healthy, the quantity or more, the quantity of times I ate daily, was the detriment that was calling my health downwards in a dark spiral leading only to demise.

Lonely I grew, cold at night, clutching the idea of life.

I struggled to feel happy my whole life, though none I would imagine would share this view of me.
I hid me feelings as well as I could shovel my food.

I hid my attempts to end my life as well as I hid the damage, I took from the one I vowed myself to.

My life had spiraled in the worst of ways, and I needed to step down with my right foot.
I needed to make a change. For myself. For my family. For my cats.

What hurts me daily was the weight I carried heavily around with me on my body,
Every day slowing my time clock more as it deterred.
This weight was detrimental to my loved ones as well.

My cats felt my pain as I was not the only one the devil tormented in our home hell hole.
I was too unfit to even stand up for them until I could defend myself.

The feeling of impending doom being trapped by a partner who is controlling to extremes.
Obsessive is an understatement when compared to this level of psychosis.

Damaged, I went to change. In an extreme way I knew I needed.
I went for the classes.

I learned all the rules.
I followed the guidelines and lost the starting requirements.

I started either losing hope or gaining courage as I grew stronger with weight finally dropping.

My determination was showing. My pants were dropping.
My doctor's office called two weeks after my first dog, Cassie.
I love you still my hound.
You dug me clear and pushed me through and yes,
You know I wanted to have the best life with you.
It tore my heart to bring you back.

I still have the videos, the memories and love in my heart
As I drop tears thinking and thanking you for being an extra motivator in my life.

You were the wagging tail that chased my cats with love and cuddles,
Unlike my partner who would drop them in the trash.

I was always on high alert, but you stepped up to the plate that day you walked out the door a dog,
Coming home with me a buddy.
Broken….
Alive…
Trying…

ring
ring
ring
ring

Always hated answering phones as I picked up the dial tone.

To my surprise, a process that normally takes six months at least, I was able to set in motion in four.

It was my gastric bypass surgery date. It would be less than a week until I would have limits that would be a harm in my eyes for my Cassie hound for, I still had the devil by my shoulder.

I did not ever want to inflict this new loving puppy to any kind of harm.
As I made the dates and set the plans, I spent my last night with my first own puppy best friend.

I cried as I called the local rescue and asked as for advice as what to do.

I knew in my heart I wanted the best for you.
We held each other into the wee morning and walked as the sun rose through the green meadow fields and the birds flew high as you sniffed then pooped and we walked slowly by.

What was sad was we worked so hard to daily walk that loop. I remember I had a tough time going once around at your pace when we met.
By our goodbye, we were timing ourselves, we were starting to run.
You added an extra bounce under each of my steps.
I miss your beefy puppy breath. The sounds of water that remind me to replenish as your tongue gulps.

The drive was short but long as it filled with tears as we talked and shared our last drive together.
We parked in the dirt lot as I hollowed inside, and I swallowed down my gulp of shame.
Unbuckled your leash and opened my door.
Came around and took you out as we slowly turn to walk into the establishment where I met you first.

It was the saddest goodbye I have ever had to say because if we had not said goodbye, who knows if either of us may be alive to say or lick hello.

To you Cassie, my puppy guardian, I thank for my great growth in confidence and strength.

To my life I respect now.
To this I say because in those times before I had that hope lift,
I had a few times were crying myself to sleep at night,
Where munching my stress away with desserts,
Or watching a Disney movie for it's all fake and can't hurt,
When all of that still was no help to my soul,
There were times I tried to leave my pains here.

I tried to slice my throat so I could never slice cake the same way again.
Nothing would go down a throat once severed.
I was stopped by my devil.
Only thought was in my mind because he didn't want to be blamed for that.
Though read my notes and the answers would have shown to be my sorrows.
The devil was a contributor too though for sure.

I tried to drive my first car to a local Walgreens and was waiting for an exact same car as mine to drive by the road and I was standing waiting to walk out in front of it.

Thankful I am now that my attention span never lasted longer than 15 minutes to dwell in any emotion.

The last time I came the closest was when I was alone for a first in my life.
After I lost my weight to be healthy,
After I completed my goal of freeing myself from that trapped deal I made with the devil,
After finally now turning my life the direction, I had wanted,

I somehow almost lost it all.
In a closet I had laid myself down.
Drowning in tears and alone I felt for too many years.

The image of myself I see in the mirror is one I feel I have no memories with.
Who am I and why do I not see the real me is still right here?

I may have dropped three hundred pounds and gained one hundred fifty to have a total new me by the end of all of the chaotic misery I so endured to get here.

Before my eyes wished to say anything with hope,
I was ready to give up.
I was drowning myself in sorrows and grabbing any ideas to ease my end of life.

I had taken a bag.
Simple a grocery bag.
The kind they warn to keep away from children due to risk of suffocation.

It works. I can't deny. I took two or three. I may not remember correctly anymore.
I remember tying the knot around my neck.
Tying tightly to make sure I couldn't remove myself.
This was my goal. My purpose in this moment.
To remove myself.

I ended up coming the closest I now wish I never knew.
My eyes, they closed.
My head lay down and my breathing had slowed.

My heart beating, harder, faster and stronger.
As if beating its prayers for me to wake and live longer.

As if a final breath could have been gone, I awoke, sweating, shaking, tearing at the bag covering my mouth.
My whole head felt like a tomato that had been perched in the sun and about to explode from the pressure held within its flush skin.

Breathe!
BREATHE!
Please let me tear this bag off my head!
I'm sorry! I'm sorry! I won't do it again!
I almost died and it was my own eyes that couldn't see the me I worked to bring the best side out of.

My whole life turned after I woke from that close demise.

I went fishing a few days later, in hopes for a bright light to guide me back away from the tunnel I almost followed too far to return from.

That chance I took on you, as scary as the chance I took on myself.

I pushed myself out of my comfort to be what society told me I needed to be if I wanted to be a happy me.
I lost all of who I looked like and now that shell of a hungry but empty being,
Is now filled with an enthusiastic and thankful woman who thanks the sky for rising each day.

Food brought me to smile when I could not walk.
You help me dance with no worries because everyone around is all Freddie Mercury and the rest is you and me just doing our well-oiled natural machine routine.
So, to judging a person for their looks, just knowing this I shared from my pained years for any to hear,
Will you speak your nasty words if you may know they can hurt as much as a knife.

Wouldn't earth be nice if we could hold our tongue from speaking harsh words and rather shared views relative to the beauty of life, we can further ensure potential positive reflections around as well.

The weight we carry within, will present itself exteriorly more often than not.
We are what we eat.

Be proud of yourself and take care of your life.
We only get one shot and worries will shorten our time.

Love your beautiful self.
Ignore what you have no control over.
The war we fight outside should be fought inside.

How is That So

I wanna see our bleachers
Splattered with the blood of our past speakers
Making the way for the future leaders
To redirect all the fucked up crap
That ended our world up in this stupid dilemma.

What is this thing called life?
Is there a lemon law to help
Guide us by shedding some light?

Today's the day when we will start to see
Everybody pay for their human greed
And teach them all the true meaning of need.

Live and never forget
Life can have no regrets

Learn, but don't look back
And goodness, show everyone equal respect.

Taking that crap no more;
No more for sure.
I'm turning and walking out that door and
Hoping nobody has to deal with the drama of
this world no more.
Space is faced with Earth's disgrace for humans
see every other species living in what we
somehow see as "our space."

It's a planet we must all live on as one and to
declare anything solely yours is completely
wrong showing plainly that us humans just don't
truly belong.

Today's the day we need to see
Everybody pay for their unnecessary greed
And all learn the true meaning of need.

Live and never forget
Life can have no regrets
Learn, but don't look back
And goodness, show everyone equal respect.

Take crap no more;
No more for sure.
I'm turning and opening a brand new door and

Hoping nobody has to deal with the drama of this world no more.

Who's the one behind the master plan to run each person's hopes and dreams into the already overflowing gutters soaked with the tears and sweat from each person who's been working their asses off for nothing to be given to them that they deserve? Not even proper respect?

What is wrong with this place?
Why don't you get your brain fixed?
Fucking shit, man!
How did this all happen?

LoL

Wouldn't that be funny?
Watch the world going up in smoke while every damn bloke and fucking dick-head is sitting in their top chambers all snug as a bug like getting a nice warm fireplace hug?

Well ignite that shit up in flames and we'll all stand on our feet that are toughened by the years of being trained for this by the system's abuse since birth having no true options.

Screwed around every other corner just looking for the relief from this shady society.

This is what we have to do.

Group together as one and take what we deserve for our futures to be able to shine like the lights in the street when the world is all in a fight and nobody knows how to make anything right.

Are we gonna lay down in a tomb??

Or what are you gonna do?

We need to fight the system once and for all or there will be nothing left worth fighting for at all.

Today's the day we need to see
Everybody with no need for grief
And all learn to lend a hand when you can.

Live and never forget
Life can have no regrets
Learn, but don't look back
And goodness, show everyone and everything love and respect.

Fight for the world.
Fight for your world.
Picture that perfect place where there is no 'better' because we are all truly in this together.
We need to stand up against the system that's kept us all captive and is designed to keep us all in line.
We need to show that 1% the extent of what they have done to their entire companies and communities throughout their existence completely blinded from their true reflection in the mirror through which we see them with our eyes.

Fighting for freedom again?

It's the time my friend.

Thirst has no chance.
The fate is in our hands.

Live and never forget
Life can have no regrets
Learn, but don't look back
And goodness. . . . . RESPECT.

Views Turning Positive

As we grow older and age through time, moving slows with each new step.
As the saying goes, either to use your body or lose it.
More to be added to the saying lists:
Keep it simple stupid.
If we all were to lose track of what in which we physically have the control over and what we mentally crave to control but in which we can never do is when madness turns to consume our soul.

So, to grow old in a world where once, mean words were kept by holding tongue and anger was settled with bullets shot out from barrels of our guns;

When all of the fighting from war is done, the sun rises to us again and the lives that were living and livid before may now be those whose souls lost to the fight. May they finally rest in peace.
What was the fight for? In the end, is there any reason we need to continue to be a world where words are not enough?
How far away is the silent treatment?
If that means peace treaty or human extinction, either is possible.

Plausible to say, that views and words are so easily construed when interpreted from one mind to the next as there may be many hidden languages of meaning to a person's sentence.

All of life in which one person experiences, is never comparable to another soul's outlook post life's experience.

This to me holds the key to why I both love and despise the expression of asking another to try to "walk in another's shoes."
This is entirely impossible as we look at one life as every day to day aspect and we realize that

each person to person interaction, each meal, every breath, all steps taken or not and down to each blink of our eyes.

No way is it ever going to be possible to fully emphasize the experience of another person's life through their personal views.

As this would lead a conclusion that seems that personally, we are a unique ecosystem of the most extreme type of life form where we are all atomically individual walls with each their own set frame of working or shutting down.

Their setups are all close in main stem in design. But to compare is not possible from one mind to the next as the exact same feeling that understands the exact stem of a single memory, view or thought can create.

So relate or negate, choose to be happy at least..

If I were to be in the views to needing anything in my life for basics, two main things I live on every day:

Coffee and positivity.

I have my own superpower, I could call it.
Freedom of speech. Whatever.

Having the profound ability to perceive every single activity or event and finding the hole of light.

Turning darkness into lightness is a huge string of holding my soul's fiber intact.

So much so that all of my cooking, artworks or writing.
Any of my animal loving's, video game time or nature adventures.
None is so enjoyable if not in a positive state of mind.

And so for any current position of views to turn negative now..
The downhill slide will be a scramble that crumble many at once.

Chaos consumes when our time passes in lacking importance of valuing positive actions taken as a whole.
We live on Earth as one and shall come to demise as one when time rings for our race to fade from the view into the dusky shade of yesterdays.

A Fool For April

A fool for April

A baby born
At 9:45 in the morn'
On a Friday
In a hospital
In the heat
Of Jackson
Mississippi.

That little baby,
Born a fool
But only feeling a tool.

Nature chose this course for me
Partially as a destiny.

My life was given a new page
As my body was taken from my town
And life instantly,
Pages re-written.

Never a chance at what could have been in my natural plan.
I know I hold the pen in my hand though.
No, not god.
Not my mom or my dad.

No friend had I to learn how to appropriately cry.

Rather I write my tears from my eyes
My entire life
Wondering how can I finally feel
Alright and feel I deserved to live this
Some would call lavish life?

I did not ask for this.

I did not demand this.

But understand this language when I explain this.

I made the most of what I was dealt.

How often has your life led you to lie?

To fake yourself a little extra?
To top your day in a sprinkle way when really it was running muddy water that overflowed your tub boat.

Just most of y'all too darn embarrassed to admit to your own faults.

See from me,
The eyes of an April Fools baby.

Born and always felt as if I was an alien or a curse upon this earth.

No help was it that I had troubling thoughts and visions that mucked up my listening skills.

Forced as a kid to swallow confusion pills.

Had enough and I faked the choke down the throat.

Would go as far as I could to hide that gross slimy slender egg boat that I just never could get to smoothly slide down to my gullet.

Ended up at 26 freaking out and shaving my head.

Instead it was intended as a Netflix inspired Viking cut.
But as a person who has cut their hair and many others,
Had her barber wish for her help before he were to retire.

Wouldn't he have laughed if he saw that I learned why no guys shave their own hair?

Next time someone,
If ever,
Asks for help with shaving their head.

Just offer to do it.

No need for me to explain the pain of trying to find the right flow and shape of my own head as it buzzed away…
Down to a mullet just for fun.
Was always a dream for me.
To cut the mullet.

Not bad as a bullet after all done as I looked like Eleven in Stranger Things.

Hey, things stranger have appeared before me before.

Not many words can explain things I have visualized deep inside my brain.

Often, I wonder if I'm insane.
And clearly, others question the same of me.

But clearly, as my life,
If under analysis;
Would you see my soul never could exist
If I ended up hurting a soul who did not deserve this.

To me, morality and ethical decisions are more important that being first in your life's visions.

To be able to live,
For me is and has been a gift.

But my life, wants more that a gift for just me.

As I never asked for my gift.
And yes, this gift confuses me.

How on earth did I come to be?
For there is no father who steps forward for
claim for bringing my possibilities to surface.
My desires are to provide a better surface for
when I leave to be deserved for all to finally
enjoy together as Earth.

Have we forgotten
That back in time
All land was spanned
In connection as lined.

Pangea was claimed.

A land so famed.

No blinded by too much light I see.

For we label more than ever needed be.

We muddied our own water.

We soiled our own foil.

We bleed into the hand that fed us by extend.

Never did we truly believe we had friends.

So self-absorbent.

So undeserving.

So unwilling to listen for a moment.

Had to shout for ever to clearly get anything to ring through the cloud of ear wax cushioning so high in your ear you could sleep past a parade on a train passing by your porta potty that you just stopped in for a moment but were too buzzed to relax in the morning.

So anyways,

A fool by page one.
My story was already sung.

Nobody believes in a joke when they learn how they started life on this earth.

Rather, the pain of mistakes made by others living beside me.

Those mistakes, made so violently.

They currently,
And coincidentally,
And sadly,

Always will hold me in by bars to my heart.

Family is and family has
Been a treasure in my life.

But wondering why my life,
Was placed away from those who knew my
chances for survival were easiest with anyone
who knew my medical bill could never be filled
by blank pages and loose spaces that never get
filled in.

A battery full of charge.

Questioning authority
Was not my intent.

I never spent even a cent
To try to disrespect the name
Of anyone else living their life
On this planet.

Even if I don't agree
With every view between
Say me and you.

Does never mean that what said is dumb.

But nearly, learn from time and time to come.

Learn that any dumb
Is only dumb if continues to be done.

Insanity is doing the same thing over and over again and expecting a different result.

By definition, a person can do as they choose.

But win or lose,
Did you have fun or was time wasted as you rushed too hard to be number one?

You're nothing if you're not the best.

If you're not first your last.

Everyone may end up laughing in class.

Always afraid to pass a little blast of gas.

How ashamed are we of ourselves that we have created this society that views everything as an issue but is too gosh darn stubborn to use a fricken tissue?

Too many babies today.

None get the voice to say.

None get a choice to play.

They listen and try.

They may end up hiding away like a turtle might shy from heavy rain.

How is life so vain?
Never fair.
Not in love or war.

Not time for luck or fear.
Neither is ever truly near.

Realize, we make our pages.

Nothing incredible happens without it being first perceived as either imaginary, impossible or too fantastical.

Life is mystical
And meant to be lived as a majestic journey.

Has your pain left you to bet your soul
To the toll of the devil to hold
And use your body as a carcass
For the darkness's bidding
To spread through too many

Festering heads?

Lay down at night to rest in bed.

Night time comes and sheep count for me.
Work those legs as they jump the fence.

Fluffy suites of wool.
Grey and white and green meadows flood my
mind each and every night.

Sounds of violins that nature designed
As a species that calms the space we relieve
ourselves through in the ease of duskily lit trees.

As a fool may say,
“Stop looking at me swan!”

But as well,
Questioning your self is the best way to better
yourself.

Now understanding that a person has come
To the age of 27
And time’s not done.

Yet they can claim,
With all truth to hail,
That their life story,

Has told no lies of tales.

They have looked inside and realized,
As a baby crying,
And as a leaky bathtub could be,
There could be no fulfillment in the spread of a lie from my lips.

The pain as it slips.

Never to my lips could I hold a secret.

These words could never be kept beneath it.

For a poker face,
One could say I show a disgrace.

But yet, yee of little faith for far too many have passed to play a poker game with me and challenge their stakes on the humiliation they expect if I fail in their eyes.

Has one ever been too honest that confusion is mainly the most common thing to pursue after the moment is passed?

Has the ice lead to rice?

And the dabs helped to ease stress at night?

Well, as holidays come and holidays go.

My own day is that of April Fools.
And no pranks too cruel from me as a little ghoul.

Always brought baked goods to school.
Kids grew to call me sweets
Even on the streets.

Though somehow, my bus seat.
Empty.

My friend list

Vacant.

I had no plans on how to spend my summer vacations.

My middle school graduation.

Teacher accommodation.

"Care" was always there to offer a hug to anyone in need. She has a strong sense of self.

So as to me a child. I know I love others always more than myself.

Questioning my reason for not feeling worthy of this opportunity as I wondered why I wasn't good enough to feel chosen as a gift by my own mother who had already birthed and kept others.

Anyways, cheese is what brings me cheers.
And eventually learned to relax and appreciate the beers.

Life is a tale.
Don't slip and slide down a scale.

Weighing yourself is for gloomy days.

When do you feel it's needed to constantly worry over things unneeded.

How has life become this heated?

April fools for a day as born by this earth.
Yet a fool could be saved as a fool can laugh freely at themselves.

Simplicity of character is the most profound of qualities.

How hard are we all laughing as we continue life
as slaves?

I promise, this is better, but yet still,
Missing a link to help this earth.

As I guarantee this was not
The master plan of honest
Abraham Lincoln.
He would not believe farther than my eyes can
see.
He would consider that we are still slaves.

But rather by oppression or by unjust force and unruly voice.

No, here.

We have a choice.

We have the right.
We have today and we have the gift of light.

Pages need to be written right. Or no point in reading them to instruct anyone right.

If school must be taught as such, than rather teach anything from the past, teach our current children and the future generations the moral

code and the profits of proper ethical reasoning
through life.
Realizing the importance of "ying and yang" for
both are needed together to equally provide
balance.

Sun and moon.
Birth and death.

Smiles and frowns.
Mountains and towns.

rock and water.
Paper and scissors.

Help finally
Learn how to
Efficiently
And effectively
Live together.

Is it all for one?
Or one for all?

What would your answer be if this
Question were asked to you?

If you decided the fates of every life back on earth?

Do you believe in every soul having worth at least in the face that they are breathing life on and thus back into this earth?

A small point can end an entire planet if Horton stops listening and caring for Who's like you's.

APRIL FOOLER HAS A BONUS POEM HERE TOO FOR YOU:

Behind closed doors:

An early morning baby
Born to win or lose.
Battle up-head was destined
For this baby of April Fools.

Life lessons,
Teach fast,
When a day to celebrate,
Becomes a joke to live through.

When words mean nothing
Because proper language
Is now reversed in meaning by
Nonsense slang terms.

The world would go to chaos
And the water claim all souls,
If we all take no time
To think of our actions
Correlating responses and consequences.

World will not last forever.
Neither should we ask or expect it to.

We do not need nor deserve to live forever
either.

Ashes to ashes.
Dust to dust.

What we do with our life once born,
Is not entirely in our hands.

When the world of opportunities
Was never laid for equality;
Though back in history we read
About famous men in wigs
And slaves on buses.

We read of farmers and maids,
Bartenders and book-keeps.

We have many of history

In all our veins.

The one thing that will always remain
Is the question of why?
Why are we here?
Why is there war?
Why does anybody lie to anyone else?
Why does anybody need to plot or scheme against others?
Why can't we actually get along?
Or at least agree to behave civilized?
Is that too much after 4 billion years of life evolving?
To expect that maybe a kind of race,
Would realize that if all fears another overpowering themselves,
And rationally continues to overlook and so preserve,
Then sudden doom may find a lost face of that fear again.

As simply as our creating a life of our own that is not of our own.
Creating birth through our life. That is a risk we can take as a race.
We have done damage when assuming if we risk the mass production
Of an alternative intelligent life form of stronger mechanisms

Than that of our soft and meaty exteriors.

We arm thick headed and big minded.
Cold hearted and shouldered.
We are close minded and blinded.

To see past the judgement we place on others for a mistake,
We may be happy once and for all.

To at the end say,
It's all okay.
And to learn from a mistake.
To understand the mistake and why is the only important difference
Between a mistake being of value or virtue.

The life we lead:
Many overlook that they have it good.

I think every time I can about how lucky and
Grateful that I have what I have and have had in my life.

I always try to see the pain it could bring
If one thing were to just dissolve from our lives.

The ability to eat.
The ability to clean.

The freshness and quality of water
And the virtue of a safe a stable home or shelter
from the weather.

If we stopped the biggest greedy members of our
world's society,
And no, not harmed them.
But made them, even unwillingly,
But for betterment of all humanity,

Give some property up for shelter spaces.
For rehabs and safe zones.

Some regularly vacant Airbnbs?
Could these not become emergency safety
zones?

If a life was fluttering in front of your eyes,
And you were blind to who they were or could
be,
But you were empathetic to their helplessness
And endangered situation…

Would you really,
Be as bad or cruel as some members played on a
tv screen?

Could you look a soul,

Climbing up your steps in the rain of a cold
harsh blizzard,
And just brittle but fighting to be alive.

Would you look that face in the eyes and choose
for yourself to put them out of their misery that
you are witnessing,
Or are their still souls of kind intentions that
May see a soup to warm and a blanket for
warmth.

A warming bucket for their feet and a night's
sleep would do them fine.

Just a simple helping of back in times how
generations hand me down their pains.
Often overlooking the goodness in days of our
lives.

Or past members of all of our times.

Our Earth In Pain

Our Earth in pain
Living our lives in vain.

Life of past on plains
Dreams gone by of happy days.

Grass always seems greener
Than our eyes imagine here.

Travel and claim
All as taken,
Even if we're the ones mistaken.

What eyes see often leads desire to follow suit to take, warning of the internal moral compass we lack to often to listen to called our conscience.

The faces of those who have lived their lives
bundled and wound up so far that a ball could
not even fly through those webs our minds
trapped within our tangled words we spew out as
too few are often found to be true.

How sad to see blankness where genuine
personality.
Used to account for the loss of empathy for
respecting the virtues of life are now lacking
through lost morality or any sense of care.

Was this ever contemplated in mind
The worst mistake from human kind?

As well as our lustful
Desires to create chaos with no foot to brake.

Simple ways
Is not always best,
For to
Dress less is
Perceived
To under
Impress the rest.

To have what we
Needed rather than
To imagine what we

Could ever dream
To want more than
The idea of time
In itself.

Life… the only thing you can't produce on a shelf.

We destroy surroundings.
We dissolve inner hopes.

Eventually destroying ourselves from within as well.

The shames.

Loss of grace.

Losing hope in saving face.

Money places smiles downgrade from general people for
Over lives are worthless for the few people in power
To best enjoy their bonus miles and a scalding shower.

Have you stopped?

In any moment?
Looking at yourselves?

Every act you make and how it corresponds to an outcome in more situations than just your own?

Imagine the tolls of the actions you laid,
Yet negligently continued to pursue ventures of own pursuit?

The bills you passed.
Either by signing them into effect
Or through passing the buck down blindly in a check?

Check.
Have you lost?
All your own respect?

Check.
Have you any morals?
Or values of ethics left?

Check.
And now check mate.

Learning how to survive was not a part of the plan for Planet Blue 262.

How do you see this came out to be true?

Yes, As even I guarantee would surely ponder
and question this too.

Though the glass would be neither half full nor
empty for them to view our chaos of so which
we misconstrue.

But first, ask that to yourselves.

Has life become what in kindergarten you had
hoped it would be?

What has life been if spent focusing on being
number one?

Trucks and luck all pushed for high hopes
For some luck or a good fuck, but blasphemy
will be our shame.

Passing off our blemishes
Hidden under more layers of foundation
Than most wedding cakes have tiers of delicacy.

What do you gain when you don't respect
yourself
Enough to have courage to freely show

Your honest self comfortably to even your own eyes
In the mirror alone at night.

Animal natures remain instinctual as always being in sync.
Don't mistake this thought as it's as shallow as one may view
A drip and a leak will continue to fill and empty routinely.

Forgetting that we are the controllers of ourselves alone.
Yourself is a well in itself that will drown alone if loneliness takes grasp when light is no longer in our hopes or mind.
Your soul's light fades silently right out of sight.

Years behind our current time.
Yes.

Not yesterday, but years gone past as we still struggle to grasp.
Why is a vision of peaceful cooperation such a rageful ideation to propose that so many still may fantasize of popping the brains out of one such peace dreamers?

A man had shared his plans.

Not any man.
A judged man.
A struggling man.
A man of faith and virtues.

Who saw eye to eye that it mattered not.
When you look at any other's face and gaze upon their eyes,
How can you deny this soul the same rights you would wish to have for yourself?

He dreamed of better lands.

Of minds in time to explain the need to end our hates.

Martin Luther was a true king.
In a Junior mind maybe only the lost can foresee paths to fix the confusion of chaos we are all drowning in still.

Decades, neigh, centuries passing and our time has spent creating waste and enabling this production to pursue has sunk our hopes and as well our future.

If we care not for one another regardless of any information,

Then no wonder it should be when we look at our decaying planet.

The sadness is for the children that generations before claimed to be doing everything to help, but was any of that true?

How judgmental we are be-forth between the forces of good and cursed walking together upon this earth's surface.

Currently,

I still mainly see currency as the cause as well the correlation of much to frequent the confusion and misdirection throughout society each day.

Lost in the search for direction.

Teachers who are instructed to force upon us their lessons that are "HIS-STORY" and worthless for value to learn.

How is this proper form of introduction to a point of view that we are "supposed to share", as knowledgeable worth for this earth to take and make work?

Time.
What is this worth?

Time?
Money on the books?
Worth what we mistook?
Time?
Lost in time?
Losing more time?
Or fading away in mindlessness?

Entertainment is a loss of spatial consciousness.

Standing there feeling empty in the brain
pondering if we're communally going silently
insane.

No further comments are coming from your
thoughts.

All lost in the viewing made to capture you.

Controlled and observed and organized by your
likes.

You lent your interests for your mind to leave
and die in the leaves you raked and left outside.

Laying there awake today.

Today could be your last day awake.

Would that be a carefree day for you as imagined?

Die to the tube you could not find haste to unglue from?

Is this the fate we have succumbed to be eternally doomed from?

The lost eyes to the blue lights that stole too fast our souls and time tells our tales now through these fake scenes we live to joke through.

Nothing spoken now is perceived and such taken as genuine anymore.

No air is clean, and no children laugh without an internal learned fear.

How dismally the gospel sounds are to be heard for a feather beating in the wind from the wings flapping under the weight of the bird taking its flight.

Any more final words?

Earth turns Blue as Sun Strikes through mistaken clouds of pain flooding the sky from one shaken troubled night when too much has been taken in spite or wrongfully from fists of might.

Indubitably So

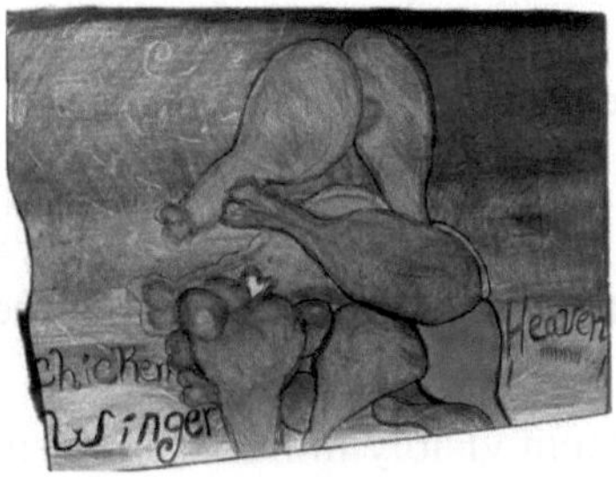

I'm undeniably the most incoherent to listen to.

Even my momma told my teachers my voice had an annoying cadence to it.

How hard is that to learn as an adult,
That your mom was never there to listen to your problems
Because your spoken words were breathy in fluency and spoken in a way that seems to ring differently.

Anyways, that's all pages from yesterday.

Today though my story goes as far to the 72 hours before.

Sleeping comes to me as a mystery.
My eyes close easily when my mind is peaceful.

At rest feels better than struggling in in-fluxing weather polar systems.

I count sheep when falling to sleep.

No literally, the old saying of counting sheep;
That's what I trained myself to fall asleep to.

Picturing them visibly in front of me each night
As I fade the pictures from my eyes that I hold open extra wide.

Dry them eyes by holding tight and count them each and every night.
Picture them in bows and hats,
All in wool covering their fat.

Jumping by themselves gets tiring to view after 6 or 7 of you.

So then a pair or two jump together,
Still counted individually as you watch them hurdle over that jump you have in every mind the same jump for them to jump each and every time.

So after the sheep have put me to sleep,
The dreams come and I can remember some.

I know that the other night I couldn't stop
staring and feeling my skin-tight ribs as I lay in
bed,
Partially afraid of my mind's abilities
Paired with my body's failing capabilities.

My slumber was hot and I the path I remember,
As my eyes behind the scenes were being led by
wolves of 3.
There they were and me a skeleton.
Walking through woods in the dark of the night.

Leading me to a tree I know.

A tree of map that is as well on me.

I photographed this the few nights before in a
space I feel is more haunted than I feared before.

Hallways and tunnels and door at the end

Opened it and it let me in.

My eyes behold a scenery of the future I hope
for peace to bring.

The day went by the next day filled with
struggles within and hopeless feelings.

Drinking the beers fills supplies for cheers
Even when weather is wilder than past years.

So the night ended well and my slumber smoothly shifted into for I fell into a laboratory instantly upon falling to sleep.
I stayed in this lab my whole night. I remember studying and experimenting to try to make everything just right.

I awoken to the freezing burr left by the ac by the door.

Got up and went to take a bath to warm my bones from their cold path.

I found the answer within my dream,
To the world's hunger issues and space travel needs.

We honey-fy everything.

Extracting nutrients can also make medicines.

The demand would be so much less if we learned to use nutrients smarter not harder or longer.

The honey-fication process is an evolutionary design that is so simple yet resourceful in my mind.

Awoken in my bath as my senses took deep breaths. My soul was aligned as I somehow floated atop the bath tub water.

I freed my sins and past disturbances.

I let go of my fear of failure again.

I wrote my pages from my mind and scribbled words out of line.

Food distractions end my thoughts in a combustion of explosions like a train stuck through a bottle line in time.

Again I know; better days ahead.
Again I know. We are never truly alone.

If a person is talking in a room and there's nobody near to hear it, it does not mean their words are not spoken. Their voices chose to use tone for a reason.

Father's Day Parade

As we look back over time
We find ourselves wondering .....
Did we remember to thank you enough
For all you have done for us?
For all the times you were by our sides
To help and support us .....
To celebrate our successes
To understand our problems
And accept our defeats?
Or for teaching us by your example,
The value of hard work, good judgment,
Courage and integrity?
We wonder if we ever thanked you
For the sacrifices you made.
To let us have the very best?
And for the simple things
Like laughter, smiles and times we shared?
If we have forgotten to show our

Gratitude enough for all the things you did,
We’re thanking you now.
And we are hoping you knew all along,
How much you meant to us.

9 789358 312935

Printed by Libri Plureos GmbH in Hamburg,
Germany